SEA SLUG

By Janie Scheff

Minneapolis, Minnesota

Credits
Cover and title page, © Sonja Ooms/iStock; 3, © Chris/Adobe Stock; 4–5, © Carlos Fernandez-Cid, carloscies/Wikimedia Commons; 7TL, © Sakis Lazarides/iStock; 7TR, © Divelvanov/iStock; 7BL, © Bruce/Adobe Stock; 7BR, © Tricie Chua/iStock; 8, © Irina K./Adobe Stock; 9, © T Karen N. Pelletreau et al./Wikimedia Commons; 11, © Timothy/Adobe Stock; 12–13, © joebelanger/iStock; 14–15, © EyeEm Mobile GmbH/iStock; 17, © Francesco Ricciardi/iStock; 19, © Eduardo/Adobe Stock; 20, © shoma81/Adobe Stock; 21, © David Salvatori / VWPics /Alamy; 22T, © A Mokhtari/iStock; 22B, © Muhammad khaleeq/iStock; 23, © Oksana/Adobe Stock.

Bearport Publishing Company Product Development Team
Publisher: Jen Jenson; Director of Product Development: Spencer Brinker; Editorial Director: Allison Juda; Editor: Cole Nelson; Editor: Tiana Tran; Production Editor: Naomi Reich; Art Director: Kim Jones; Designer: Kayla Eggert; Designer: Steve Scheluchin; Production Specialist: Owen Hamlin

Statement on Usage of Generative Artificial Intelligence
Bearport Publishing remains committed to publishing high-quality nonfiction books. Therefore, we restrict the use of generative AI to ensure accuracy of all text and visual components pertaining to a book's subject. See BearportPublishing.com for details.

Library of Congress Cataloging-in-Publication Data is available at www.loc.gov or upon request from the publisher.

ISBN: 979-8-89577-047-4 (hardcover)
ISBN: 979-8-89577-471-7 (paperback)
ISBN: 979-8-89577-164-8 (ebook)

Copyright © 2026 Bearport Publishing Company. All rights reserved. No part of this publication may be reproduced in whole or in part, stored in any retrieval system, or transmitted in any form or by any means, electronic, mechanical, photocopying, recording, or otherwise, without written permission from the publisher. Bearport Publishing is a division of FlutterBee Education Group.

For more information, write to Bearport Publishing, 3500 American Blvd W, Suite 150, Bloomington, MN 55431.

Contents

Awesome Sea Slugs! 4
So Many Slugs......................... 6
Colorful Camouflage.................... 8
Scaring Off Danger 10
Toxic Thieves 12
Hunting for Food 14
Solar Powered! 16
Sea Slug Families 18
Slow and Short Lives 20

Information Station 22
Glossary 23
Index 24
Read More 24
Learn More Online 24
About the Author 24

AWESOME
Sea Slugs!

A rainbow blob ripples in the water as it slowly makes its way along the ocean floor. **SQUELCH!** The vibrant sea slug leaves behind a slimy trail everywhere it goes. Colorful and squishy, sea slugs are awesome!

> SIMILAR TO A LAND SLUG, A SEA SLUG'S SLIME HELPS IT STICK TO THINGS.

So Many Slugs

There are more than 3,000 **species** of sea slugs in the world's oceans. Most live near the coasts, but some have been found in the deep sea. All sea slugs are **mollusks**. Like most mollusks, sea slugs have squishy bodies and breathe through **gills**. But unlike other mollusks, sea slugs do not have hard outer shells.

> WHILE MOST SEA SLUGS GET AROUND BY CRAWLING ON THE OCEAN FLOOR, SOME FLOAT IN THE OPEN WATER.

Gills

Colorful Camouflage

Sea slugs come in many shapes, sizes, and colors. Some use their appearance for **camouflage**. They share a color, pattern, or texture with the things in their watery home. This helps them hide from **predators** looking for a snack.

SOME KINDS OF SEA SLUGS LOOK LIKE FLOATING SEAWEED!

Scaring Off Danger

While some sea slugs hide to stay safe, others use their coloring to send a warning. **BEWARE!** Colorful bodies tell predators that these slugs are dangerous. Many sea slugs have toxins that cause sickness or even death when eaten. Others have cells full of venom that sting when touched. Predators know to avoid these dangerous slugs.

> SOME PREDATORS, SUCH AS SEA STARS, ARE NOT AFFECTED BY SEA SLUG TOXINS OR STINGS.

Toxic Thieves

Where do sea slugs get their toxins or stinging cells? The slugs eat foods with these deadly defenses. While most other animals are hurt or killed by these creatures, sea slugs take in their venom or toxins. They store the substances within their bodies for later use.

Hunting for Food

Most sea slugs use special hornlike tentacles on their heads to sense and smell their **prey**. *SNIFF!* They also have teeth like cheese graters. When a sea slug finds a tasty meal, such as a jellyfish or **anemone**, it grabs it with its teeth and begins to shred apart the feast.

SEA SLUGS ARE OFTEN THE SAME COLOR AS THE FOOD THEY EAT.

Solar Powered!

While sea slugs are animals, some can make food like plants! These sea slugs feed on **algae** and absorb their **chloroplasts**. This helps the slugs use sunlight to make energy through **photosynthesis**. Sea slugs with chloroplasts can go without eating for more than nine months!

THE LEAF SHEEP SEA SLUG IS ONE OF THE FEW ANIMALS THAT CAN MAKE ENERGY FROM THE SUN.

Sea Slug Families

The ocean is big, so it can be tough for sea creatures to find a **mate**. Luckily, sea slugs are helped along by a couple of factors. These creatures release a smelly chemical to get others' attention. Also, since each sea slug is both male and female, they can mate with any other slug of their species. Once two sea slugs mate, both lay eggs in a strand covered in jelly. **SLIMY!**

SOME SEA SLUGS LAY JUST A FEW EGGS AT A TIME, WHILE OTHERS LAY MILLIONS AT ONCE.

A strand of sea slug eggs

Slow and Short Lives

After about 50 days, sea slug eggs hatch into babies called **larvae**. Most larvae are on their own right away. They eat and grow into adults after only a few months. Adult sea slugs live for up to four years, spending their time eating, mating, and brightening up the ocean floor.

MOST SEA SLUG LARVAE HAVE A HARD OUTER SHELL THAT THEY LOSE SOON AFTER THEY HATCH.

Information Station

SEA SLUGS ARE AWESOME!
LET'S LEARN MORE ABOUT THEM.

Kind of animal: Sea slugs are mollusks. All mollusks have soft bodies without spines. Most have hard outer shells.

More mollusks: There are almost 100,000 species of mollusks. Octopuses and squids are two other kinds that do not have shells.

Size: The largest sea slugs can be 1 foot (0.3 m) long. That's as long as two dollar bills.

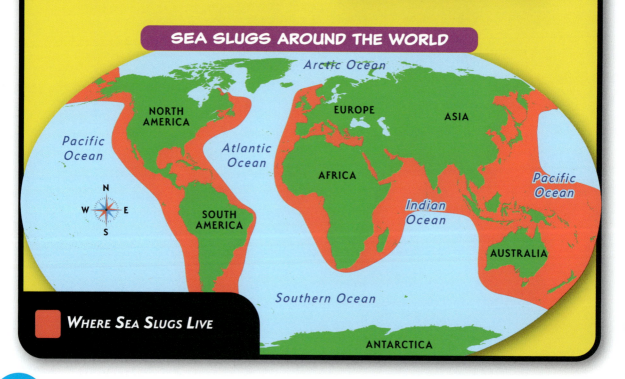

SEA SLUGS AROUND THE WORLD

■ Where Sea Slugs Live

Glossary

algae plantlike living things that can make food from sunlight through photosynthesis

anemone brightly colored sea animals with tube-shaped bodies and tentacles

camouflage to disguise oneself in order to blend in with the surroundings

chloroplasts tiny cells in plants that change sunlight into energy

gills organs that help some animals breathe under water

larvae the young form of certain animals

mate a partner to have young with

mollusks animals with soft bodies, no spines, and that are often protected by hard shells

photosynthesis the process plants use to make food using water, carbon dioxide, and sunlight

predators animals that hunt and eat other animals

prey an animal that is hunted and eaten by other animals

species groups that animals are divided into, according to similar characteristics

Index

algae 16
camouflage 8
chloroplasts 16
gills 6
larvae 20
mate 18
mollusks 6
photosynthesis 16
predators 8, 10
prey 14
tentacles 12–14
toxins 10, 12

Read More

Owen, Ruth. *Animal Camouflage in the Ocean (Hide to Survive!).* Minneapolis: Lerner Publishing Group, 2024.

Salvatore, Kaitlyn. *Mollusks (Discover More: Marine Wildlife).* Buffalo, NY: Britannica Educational Publishing, 2025.

Learn More Online

1. Go to **FactSurfer.com** or scan the QR code below.
2. Enter "**Sea Slug**" into the search box.
3. Click on the cover of this book to see a list of websites.

About the Author

Janie writes books for kids and lesson plans for teachers. She loves nature hikes and taking her three kids to the zoo!